You can excel beyond yourself.

A useful manual to help you Excel, flourish and be better.

Jeffrey P. Parker

Table of content

Chapter 1

Introduction

The desire to be happy and the desire to feel content with life are the two things that people most commonly want. Think about attempting to instill these 10 straightforward attributes inside yourself to reach these goals and to experience great satisfaction and personal satisfaction in your life and career:

1. Be genuine.

Be genuine. Let the outcomes of your life demonstrate how open you are to using your freedoms. Be sure to express your independent thought, free will, and self-will. Live from your individuality and willingness to stand out from the crowd. Your authenticity is that part of yourself that is secure and true enough to endure the damaging external pressures that frequently arise from life and business.

When you are authentic to who you are and deeply committed to your life, you choose to see options over an obstacle. Because every path you take in life, both personally and professionally, is entirely consistent with who you are, your actual essence is not concealed behind pretenses.

2. Be sincere.
The importance of honesty to your life and business cannot be overstated. Ask yourself how lying has ever benefited anyone, including yourself, to have a better understanding of why being honest is crucial. Your reputation is the one thing you simply cannot afford to lose. If it is misplaced by dishonesty, it might be impossible to get it back.

Living by the truth enables you to develop trustworthy connections with your family, friends, coworkers, rivals, employees, and clients. Your candor inspires those around you, motivating them to develop their professional and personal relationships with you moving ahead.

3. Make an effort.
Challenge yourself to get the most out of your life and profession. By remaining with what is safe and familiar, you will never be able to achieve even a small portion of your dreams.

Nothing is requiring you to rise to the occasion and reach your potential where there is security. Encourage oneself to always go after challenging objectives. That illusive "thing" that drives you to engage in life in ways that you wouldn't if you were secure and comfortable must be present for you to set out to accomplish those goals.

Your confidence grows when you push yourself and succeed, making it easier for you to take on new challenges. You increase your self-confidence by taking on challenges, which also help you advance your knowledge and skills.

4. Prioritize love.

Those that care about you are the most important people in your life. These are the people you can depend on no matter how much the outside world has let you down. The people that provide the greatest worth to your world are those who adore and embrace you despite your flaws and shortcomings and do not require you to be different. When you cannot, they assist in reviving your confidence in yourself.

Nothing could ever compare to the love that these people show you in terms of money. They give you a sense of community and belonging, which makes life more enjoyable and satisfying. People who do not place a high priority on their relationships are less well-rounded, happier, and more unsuccessful in life. Stop letting this be you.

5. Think carefully.

Give everyone you interact with a sense of respect and worth. Another person will be inspired to uphold their sense of importance if you can help them feel that way. You are not a pushover if you are considerate of other people. Being thoughtful in all of your interactions is that high-level attribute of being emotionally intelligent. When you communicate with others openly and respectfully, you can remain composed and on-topic.

Remember that being angry is never beneficial in interpersonal or professional relationships since it is very difficult to appreciate someone furious. Nobody can think clearly while they are angry.

6. Practice ethical behavior.
In the same way that you want people to be thoughtful of you, do the same for others. To create peace in your life and the world at large, practice tolerance and acceptance. Let go of narrow-mindedness, intolerance, disparaging remarks about other people, and self-righteousness.

Being tolerant is a virtue that everyone should have. Consider your place in the world or life as a whole, as well as the impact you want your actions to have. Be that bigger person, if possible. You never know what kind of individual might hold your next biggest change in his or her hands, so be open-minded to learning from all types of people and their diverse opinions.

7. Show patience.
The secret to a successful life and career is understanding the difference between patience and waiting. Waiting is not part of being patient. Waiting is passive. Even when you are not yet

seeing results, patience teaches you to never give up on your goals. You have ceased working if you are only "waiting." When you are passionate about something, there is no cap to how much work you will put in if you believe it will advance your goals.

Being patient implies having enough faith in your goals to keep moving forward.

8. Pursue your goals.

Live your dreams instead of just following them. Turn each wish into a reality. Work consistently, precisely, and resolutely to realize your dreams. What makes a life well lived is living your dreams. You will lead a life full of vitality, excitement, and the happiness you deserve if you pursue what you do with enthusiasm.

Your goals and interests provide your life—and the lives of others—deeper significance. Living your dreams makes you an inspiration. You implant in others the idea that anything is possible if it is feasible for you.

9. Have a heart of gratitude.

The bad emotional sensations of envy, victimization, and jealousy decrease as your good feelings get stronger when you have a grateful heart. Gratitude improves the quality of your memories and serves as a powerful stress-reduction tool.

Your personal and professional lives become more loving, successful, and pleasurable for you and everyone you come in contact with when you practice gratitude. It also helps you reach your life and career goals.

10. Maintain humility.

Commit to working quietly and letting your success speak for itself. The foundation of humility is introspection. But for you, it's all about other people when deciding where to direct your time and energy. Being humble means that you have the bravery to take risks and attempt new things without being self-centered or self-conscious. Because you are not bound by expectations, you are not forced to strive for perfection. Your paralysis caused by the dread of failing is broken by doing this.

Being modest allows you to approach life with flexibility and openness. Because your primary attention is not on wanting to be either successful or happy, you are not only affected by the desire for happiness or success for yourself. Instead, you become enmeshed in endeavors, hobbies, individuals, and things that you view as more significant than yourself. As a natural outcome of this, you experience greater happiness and success.

Helping people achieve the happiness and success they want is the surest way to find happiness and success in life.

You must regularly reflect on what it means to be authentic if you want to feel content, happy, and satisfied with who you are, what you are doing, and who you still want to become. To challenge yourself, face anxieties, be kind to others, and be the conscious creator of the fullness of your overall life experience, you must be committed and intentional in your pursuit.

Chapter 2

You are more than you think

Believe in yourself. You are braver than you believe, more skilled than you realize, and capable of more than you anticipate.Why you can always do more than you think you can, but won't:

You can work harder than you believe you can. But if you think you can't, you probably won't even try.You can learn faster than you believe you can. But if you think you can't, you probably won't even try.You can keep giving longer than you believe you can. But if you think you can't, you probably won't even try.You can dream greater than you believe you can. But if you think you can't, you probably won't even try.You can live more boldly than you believe you can. But if you think you can't, you probably won't even try.

You can push the limitations a little bit more than you think you can. But if you think you can't, you probably won't even try.You can dive deeper than you believe you can. But if you think you can't, you probably won't even try.You can fight through the exhaustion longer than you believe you can. But if you think you can't, you probably won't even try.You can tolerate being laughed at more than you think you can. But if you think you can't, you probably won't even try.

Chapter 3

How More compassion Wash your heart

Introduction: Practicing Kindness:

What is the first thing you tell yourself when you walk into a room full of people, join a meeting, bring up a problem, correct a child, offer a friend feedback, or tell a joke? Likewise, what do you pray about at these times? In this lesson, you will read about an important attitude that God wants us to have in all of these situations—to be kind.

Being kind implies being sympathetic and generous in your heart, thoughts, and actions. It involves being truly concerned for the welfare of others.That doesn't come naturally for most of us, especially when we are upset or frustrated. However, when we grow closer to Jesus, God wants us to change, to become gentler.

That's because kindness is one fruit of the Spirit, fruit that grows in us as we grow in Christ.How we treat our hearts is as crucial today as it is throughout the rest of our lives. Kindness affects our heart rate, our blood pressure, and the stress on our hearts. It is often claimed that we don't have control over many circumstances in our lives, but we can control our answers. Responding in a "fight or flight" fashion generally puts extra pressure on the heart along with elevated blood pressure, blood glucose, and other functions.

It takes practice but a calmer response will allow our heart rate and pressure on the heart muscle to be more relaxed. Most stressful situations spring up and pass before we know it. A motorist may cut us off in traffic, an unpleasant person may say or do something uncalled for, or we may experience anything uncomfortable. Realize that for the moment it may be alright to be upset, but to let that feeling go and be nice to your heart. "Let go and let God."Kindness: the attribute of being pleasant, generous, and caring; a kind act. In her article, "The Heart and Science of Kindness," Melissa Broderick, Med, has compiled these Kindness Tips which have been reduced to incorporate each of the topics.

Kindness Starts With Being Kind To Yourself Lead With Compassion, Follow With Kindness We Feel Happier When We Act In Service To Others Choose Kindness Give To Give, Not To Receive We Become Kinder With Practice .Kindness Begets Kindness

Kindness Is Lasting

In summation, famed novelist and speaker Maya Angelou stated possibly her most famous remark when she said, "I've discovered that people will forget what you said, people will forget what you did, but people will never forget how you made them feel."Kindness is one of the few things that will moderate the response of others. Teach kids how to demonstrate kindness to others.

Were you ever bullied on the playground? Or called names by the neighbor kid? Do you have an unpleasant co-worker? A friend who presses your buttons?When I was a kid, my mom would scold me, "Josh, kill them with kindness."The motivation behind this advice may sound harsh, but I believe it shows us something about the power of kindness. In Romans 2:4, the apostle Paul explains it this way: "God's mercy pushes you toward repentance." My mom and the apostle Paul realized the same biblical truth: Kindness can soften hearts.

The Greek root word kindness, as employed in the New Testament, denotes uprightness or benevolence and describes the ability to act for the well-being of people demanding our patience. Kindness may seem extremely unnatural, though. When we have been hurt or offended, we tend to react in wrath or bitterness. But kindness prompts us to do quite the opposite – to respond with love and forgiveness (Ephesians 4:32). (Ephesians 4:32).

Kindness is when your child, though treated harshly by a friend, shares gummy bears with his friend at snack time. Kindness is when you, however, irritated by your child's poor decisions, choose not to react in anger. It's an unnatural deed that comes supernaturally through the Holy Spirit.But kindness by itself is insufficient. Paul portrays kindness as a portion of the fruit of the Spirit, which also includes love, joy, peace, patience, goodness, faithfulness, gentleness, and self-control (Galatians 5:22-23). (Galatians 5:22-23).

He speaks of the fruit of the Spirit, however, not as a collection of distinctive character traits, but as one thing.Compassion must be accompanied by goodness. That's because compassion without goodness can become tolerant of vice — just as good without kindness can be harsh and rigid. We demonstrate the fruit of the Spirit only as we cultivate these qualities together.Children of all ages can begin to comprehend kindness from a biblical perspective.

Chapter 4

The love you deserve

One day you'll meet the love of your life when you least expect it.It doesn't matter whether you've been single your whole life or you were in a terrible relationship the entire time. It doesn't matter whether you're skeptical about love or in the wreck of your heartache. It doesn't matter if you're bubbling with confidence and radiating intense love for yourself, or mired in self-hatred and thinking you ruined your own life.None of that matters when love comes knocking at your door.It doesn't matter because there is no prerequisite to love.

No predetermined timing that you have to wait for. It could be a random day when you meet eyes with a cute stranger in the crowd. A blind date that gives you butterflies in your stomach and a nice feeling in your heart. A random encounter that proved to be the start of a developing romance.The fact about love is that you won't expect it and you won't see it coming.And maybe that's the beauty of it. Love just arrives out of the blue and surprises you at every twist and turn. It grabs you out of nowhere and alters you for the better. It leaves an impression on your life and leaves you never the same again.One day you'll fall in love and for the first time, everything feels perfect where it should be.Unlike in the past when you tended to fret and wait for the other shoe to drop, now you feel cherished and secure knowing instinctively that your partner will never hurt you.

While your thoughts used to be all over the place and you were afraid of the unknown and in a rush to find out what happens next, you're now satisfied to take things slowly and enjoy the process of getting to know your particular person.You're excited to give this new romance a go. You trust in the direction that it is heading. You begin to listen to your instinct and it urges you to follow your heart.

One day you'll discover the love you deserve and until then, have faith that you'll find it. It's okay to date with a purpose. It's acceptable if you refuse to settle down until you're ready. It's good to be alone instead of hurrying to be with someone. You're not wrong for being against casual dating. You're not at blame for being enthusiastic about love. You're not to be blamed for refusing to settle for love. You're not being utopian in expecting to find true love. Love is the one thing you should never sacrifice your values for. Never settle for someone who doesn't interest your head and stir your heart. Never accept someone less deserving of what you have to offer.You deserve your text to be replied to and someone happy to spend time with you every waking moment.

You deserve tangible promises and plans transformed into reality. You deserve a true connection and not anything vague without labels that you don't know where you stand and what it all means.You deserve someone you can be with openly and the one you proudly show off at family reunions and friend gatherings where everyone is finally happy for you. You deserve someone who brightens your life and offers you more reasons to grin every single day.

You deserve someone who you can feel in your gut and you know, this is it. One day you'll find the love you deserve and the one that is meant for you. It may be a life-changing day and you may be looking forward to it, but you aren't stressing over it.You know that it will arrive, and until then, you are satisfied to wait.

Chapter 5

Change from the Inside out

If you want to know what your thoughts were yesterday, check at your body now. If you want to know what your body will look like tomorrow, look at your thoughts today.How our Inner State influences our Physical Experience.

I have always been fascinated by the intrinsic link between our inner state of being and our bodily experience in life. It seems that there are times when all the physical effort in the world isn't enough to achieve the change we are seeking. But at the same time, sometimes a small alteration in how we think, feel or see ourselves, each other, or our situation, causes a beneficial reverberation across our physical experience that we never could have imagined.

Observing seagulls, I feel a spark of their freedom inside. Birds do not drag themselves down with things. What they have they are; at any time, in any place, ready to stay or move on. Though human beings are often described as the peak of evolution, we can learn from animals. No lion is inclined to kill and acquire more food than he needs for himself and his pride; no eagle constructs more than one nest to breed her children. Putting things into perspective, it appears that the retirement vision of many hardworking individuals curiously resembles an animalistic routine: spending time outside or with friends, enjoying sunshine and nature.

As pondered upon by the Dalai Lama, 'Man sacrifices his health to make money. Then he sacrifices his money to recoup his health. Thinking back about the past 20 years of my life, the second part of the Dalai Lama's contemplation is even more accurate: 'He is so anxious about the future that he does not enjoy the present; the result being that he does not live in the present or the future; he lives as if he is never going to die, and then he dies having never really lived.

So driven was I by the longing for something or another, that I forgot to relish the beauty of now. How lucky I am that my recent plans have not achieved the desired results. The past twelve months taught me that life is a house of cards; neatly stacked at this moment, and ready to collapse in the next when a single card is plucked out. A toppling house of cards may turn out to be the finest of gifts; a grace that one would have never dared to ask for. Had I been confronted with the perspective of my present situation a year ago I would have been frozen with worry; clutching for dear life to the status quo, frightened to lose all I had and cherished. As this book goes into print COVID-19 engulfs the World. Declared a Pandemic on March 11th, 2020, the growing disaster is a reminder that anything can change always, from one moment to the next.

It also demonstrates the serious repercussions that result when civilizations do not spend systematically to satisfy the basic social needs of everyone. 2020 portrays what happens when the interests of a few rule over the needs of many;

while the majority shy away from contemplating, and doing something, about the repercussions. The outcome of COVID-19 rests on the ability and desire of individuals and institutions to extend their vision drastically. Hopefully, the paradigm shift that is given in this book contributes to this change in dynamics.

Work to Live or Live to Work:

We grow up with the assumption that 'work' is how we contribute to society. Thinking inside this mental logic, our occupations determine us. What we do daily not only form our habits and talents, our relationships and assets, it progressively makes us who we are, at least at the surface. Consequently, our work becomes crucial in shaping the perception that we have of our worth.

What becomes the Who? In addition, even though there are extremely various working relations and constellations now, with freelancing ever-growing thanks to technology, traditionally, work placed the worker in a position inside a framework. The ordinary employee did spend more time at the workplace than at home; more time with coworkers than with family and friends. Unemployment is disturbing because, beyond the practical ramifications, it is uprooting not only treasured routines but the social norms and beliefs below; not just deleting a set of activities but the human eco-environment that they have been operated in.

However, despite and because of this profound personal commitment to our day-to-day employment, a paradoxical dynamic is at play. The What takes over the Why and the How. We fixate on the chores on our immediate radar, losing sight of the wider picture. On the other hand, though, having shrunk down our perspective so much we lose sight of the actual impact of these various micro-tasks and their interplay.

Rather than honing our focus on a relatively limited subject to provide our absolute best in this particular field, we rush from one duty to the next, much as a hamster keeps going on its wheel, step after step after step. There is always one more task, deadline, or paper to do; devouring our time and energy. Our brain space is saturated before we even start to think about what matters for ourselves.

Martin Luther King stated 'Whatever your life's job is, do it so well that the living and the dead and the unborn, could do no better. If we followed his words, there would never be the need to ponder what we should have done differently. Similarly, a major premise of Karma yoga is to give one's best, and then let go1; the effects of whatever has been done are not in the hands of the one who performed (Raju 1954). (Raju 1954).

However, since the result of our activity is no longer the center does not remove the need to offer one's best. Giving everything we have and can accomplish, in every single moment, committing our whole being, all our attention to the precise situation that we are in, the person we engage with, and the work at hand means that we do the best we can at that moment.

If you act in keeping with your beliefs, exerting all the necessary effort, and the best knowledge that you have at the time of the action, why would you blame yourself if the outcome of your action is not the intended one?

Shifting scope from future outcomes to present input does not erase accountability, rather it puts the cursor on the proper point; where we can do something about it. Life is complex and what happens involves many interwoven factors. Focusing on the now, in the understanding that the result is not in our control takes away distraction.

Not flagellating ourselves when things go wrong, nor admiring our virtues when they go well, liberates mental space that can be put to good use—like zooming in on the purpose of our occupation, the Why.

The brain appreciates simplicity. Therefore, most conversations start with inquiries like 'What do you do?' 'Where do you come from?', etc. People in boxes are easier to grasp, appraise, and categorize than free-floating electrons. Tasks are more tangible than the investigations of ambitions, emotions, or thoughts. Safe ground. Think about the last social gathering that you attended, which contained new people whom you never met before.

What do you remember from the little discussion about weather and work? Imagine how much more engaging these talks may have been if instead of asking about a person's work, you would have asked about their passion; the Why that matters to them? Hiding behind the shell of our past successes and present social status is a technique of riding on the social wave. Diving down needs a deep breath but discovering the wildlife and vegetation deep down is more than worth it.

Four Entry Points to Connect

Based on my previous experiences, from institutional membership as a source of identity to detachment this subsection introduces notions that Illustrating the continuum of extremes demonstrates the transition that might drive an individual to migrate from one side of the spectrum to the other.

How we live in this world is formed by our aspirations, our emotions, our thoughts, and our sensations. Imagine yourself as a Russian doll, a 'Matryoshka'; a doll within a doll, within a doll. Each doll is part of the next bigger one. However, unlike the traditional, physical layers of a 'Matryoshka', the four dimensions of our being are not independent entities.

They continuously interact and influence each other, engaged in a continuing spiral dynamic, from the center to the perimeter and from the periphery inwards. This internal two-way interplay determines who and how we are, what we do, and how we interact with the outside world.

Starting at the center of our being, the soul symbolizes the essence of who we are. It embodies our goal, the urge to find significance in everyday lives. Whatever we feel, think, and do is rooted in this quest for significance.

The second dimension is our emotions. Schematically and symbolically speaking, they are placed in the heart, determining how we feel in a certain situation. Emotions are crucial in determining attitudes, decisions, and behaviors. No matter how much we 'know' about a given situation, an emotional urge will set the trigger that changes our attitude from information, to understanding, to desire for change, to physical manifestation—action.4

The third component of Who we are is the mind. Our thoughts are the consequence of an intricate mixture of genetic disposition, education, beliefs, memories, upbringing, and environment; they influence our emotions and ambitions, our physical experiences and expressions; and they are influenced by them in turn.

The fourth dimension is the body, which is the outer membrane that connects and separates our internal and external realm. As an interface between the interior and the outer, it is the level on which we experience and express ourselves in it.

Nothing happens in a vacuum. The body mirrors our internal situations. Conversely, our experience of the environment affects our internal circumstances, changing our perception of the world and hence our attitude to it. Like a stone dropped into the sea, whatever happens in the middle spreads out. Whichever state our internal realm is in—our emotions and ideas which are influenced by our ambitions, effects our engagement with the outside

'The first fallacy is that it is feasible to avoid influencing people's choices (Thaler and Sunstein 2008)

Everything is interrelated, from the inside out and the outside in. Our aspirations affect our emotions, which influence our thoughts and hence our experiences and expressions (feeling)

(sensation). Conversely, how we express ourselves generates specific experiences, which result in bodily sensations that inspire thoughts and emotions, which feed or alter our goals; and shape our memories. These memories impact our emotions and thoughts in future situations, and hence our future expressions and experiences

Chapter 6

A healthy love of oneself

What is the love of oneself?

We must first comprehend what it means before we can begin to practice it.

Self-love is a feeling of admiration for oneself that develops through behaviors that promote our mental, emotional, and spiritual development. Having high regard for your happiness and well-being is what it means to love yourself. Self-love entails attending to your own needs and refraining from putting your health at risk to please others. Not settling for less than you deserve is a sign of self-love.

Since we all have a variety of ways to care for ourselves, self-love can mean different things to different people. Your mental wellness depends on you figuring out what self-love means to you personally.

What does "loving oneself" mean to you?

It can initially mean:

talking lovingly to and about oneself

Putting yourself first

Taking a break from self-criticism

believing in yourself

being honest with oneself

respecting oneself

establishing sound boundaries

accepting your shortcomings and being kind to yourself

Many individuals consider self-love to be another word for self-care. We frequently have to return to the fundamentals to engage in self-care.

Observe our bodies.

During your downtime, stretch and move around.

Put your phone down and spend time with yourself, and others, or create something.

eating a balanced diet while occasionally indulging in your favorite dishes

Self-love entails accepting yourself for who you are right now, in this very instant. It entails putting your physical, emotional, and mental health first and accepting your emotions for what they are.

How and Why to Love Yourself

We now understand that loving yourself encourages you to live a healthy lifestyle. When you value yourself highly, you're more likely to make decisions that promote your well-being and are beneficial to you. These items could take the form of a nutritious diet, regular exercise, or wholesome relationships.

What does "loving oneself" mean to you?

It can initially mean:

talking lovingly to and about oneself

Putting yourself first

Taking a break from self-criticism

believing in yourself

being honest with oneself

respecting oneself

establishing sound boundaries

accepting your shortcomings and being kind to yourself

Many individuals consider self-love to be another word for self-care. We frequently have to return to the fundamentals to engage in self-care.

How to practice loving yourself includes:

being conscious.

People who value themselves are more likely to be aware of their thoughts, feelings, and desires. acting out of necessity rather than desire.

By keeping your attention on what you need, you can avoid automatic behavior patterns that lead to mishaps, leave you mired in the past, and undermine your self-esteem.

taking good care of oneself.

When you better meet your needs, you will love yourself more. People who have a high level of self-love take care of themselves every day by engaging in healthy habits including good eating, exercise, rest, intimacy, and constructive social connections.

making way for wholesome practices.

Start genuinely taking care of yourself by doing the same for your diet, workout routine, and leisure activities. Do things because you care about yourself rather than just to "get it done" or because you "have to."

Finally, to practice self-love, start by treating yourself with the same compassion, kindness, and care that you would show to a loved one.

Chapter 7

The Unseen Advantages of Silence

There may be considerable benefits to your psychological and mental health from turning down the noise.

Do you enjoy being alone with your thoughts or do you find it repugnant?

Our noisy environment helps some people block out any unwanted thoughts that may occasionally enter their heads.

Others may benefit from some much-needed clarity after some time in solitude. You might be losing out on the benefits of silence if you occupy your free time with loud activities.

Many of us don't embrace stillness all that frequently since our lives are so busy. So how can silence assist us?

Even while it can be challenging to find quiet times, doing so may be good for both your physical and emotional health. Here are some benefits of silence:

1) Quiet promotes mindfulness

For the practice of mindfulness, which has numerous advantages for mental health, silence can serve as a prelude.

According to Sarah Kaufman, a licensed master social worker located in New York City, "being mindful and aware of what is happening in the present moment helps reduce anxiety, quiet racing thoughts, and relax the nervous system.

You can become comfortable in your body and mind and be present at the moment by practicing mindfulness. If you sense the want to mentally challenge yourself, try to refocus your attention on the peaceful, present moment.

2) Fosters awareness of oneself by allowing you to objectively observe and accept your thoughts and feelings, silence can help you become more self-aware.

You become more conscious of your body and thoughts when you're sitting quietly and unmoving. According to Kaufman, this can provide you with a wealth of knowledge that you can thoughtfully consider and try to better understand.

What emotions do you experience? Do you feel tranquil, at ease, and calm? Or are you restless, agitated, or bored?

By helping you connect with your feelings and emotions, these questions can help you find deep insights into your life.

3) Activates brain tissue

According to a 2013 mouse animal study, calming the mind can promote brain growth. Researchers discovered that mice's hippocampus created new cells when they were given 2 hours each day of stillness.

The hippocampus is the part of the brain associated with memory, emotions, and learning.

4) Reduces anxiety

We all experience stress occasionally, but quiet has the potential to reduce stress by lowering cortisol and adrenaline levels.

According to a reliable source, even two minutes of quiet might be more peaceful than soothing music. Changes in blood pressure and blood flow to the brain were thought to be the cause of this.

According to Brent Metcalf, a certified clinical social worker in Johnson City, Tennessee, when we allow ourselves to be silent, we allow our brains to simply reset and be refreshed.

This lessens the symptoms of stress and anxiety brought on by the disarray in our lives.

5) Aids in the processing of information

The brain requires time to ponder, think, and rest. It needs time to organize the knowledge it already possesses and make room for the new knowledge.

You are giving your brain the time it needs to comprehend any new information by scheduling quiet time during the day.

6. Encourages creativity

In her book "Saving Our Children From Our Chaotic World: Teaching Children the Magic of Silence and Stillness," author Maggie Dent asserts that "Creativity is a huge advantage of silence and stillness." According to Dent, for the body to be in the background and the mind to be at ease, both are necessary for the zone of inspiration. Making mental space for creativity can assist.

7) Supports mental clarity

Dr. Elizabeth Lombardo, a psychologist in Chicago, Illinois, says that silence improves focus. "The ability to focus when the modern world and its various noises bombard your brain all at once is one of the reasons why silence has become such an important element of everyday life," states one researcher.

You might find it difficult to focus with this background noise. According to Lombardo, you might be able to concentrate better in a calm setting or one with less outside noise.

Do you enjoy being alone with your thoughts or do you find it repugnant?

Our noisy environment helps some people block out any unwanted thoughts that may occasionally enter their heads.

Others may benefit from some much-needed clarity after some time in solitude. You might be losing out on the benefits of silence if you occupy your free time with loud activities.

Many of us don't embrace stillness all that frequently since our lives are so busy. So how can silence assist us?

Even while it can be challenging to find quiet times, doing so may be good for both your physical and emotional health. Here are some benefits of silence:

1. Quietness promotes attentiveness

For the practice of mindfulness, which has numerous advantages for mental health, silence can serve as a prelude.

According to Sarah Kaufman, a licensed master social worker located in New York City, "being mindful and aware of what is happening in the present moment helps reduce anxiety, quiet racing thoughts, and relax the nervous system.

You can become comfortable in your body and mind and be present at the moment by practicing mindfulness. If you sense the want to mentally challenge yourself, try to refocus your attention on the peaceful, present moment.

2. Fosters awareness of oneself

By allowing you to objectively observe and accept your thoughts and feelings, silence can help you become more self-aware.

You become more conscious of your body and thoughts when you're sitting quietly and unmoving. According to Kaufman, this can provide you with a wealth of knowledge that you can thoughtfully consider and try to better understand.

What emotions do you experience? Do you feel tranquil, at ease, and calm? Or are you restless, agitated, or bored?

By helping you connect with your feelings and emotions, these questions can help you find deep insights into your life.

3. Activates brain tissue

According to a 2013 mouse animal study, calming the mind can promote brain growth. Researchers discovered that mice's hippocampus created new cells when they were given 2 hours each day of stillness.The hippocampus is the part of the brain associated with memory, emotions, and learning.

4. Reduces tension

We all experience stress occasionally, but quiet has the potential to reduce stress by lowering cortisol and adrenaline levels. According to a reliable source, even two minutes of quiet might be more peaceful than soothing music. Changes in blood pressure and blood flow to the brain were thought to be the cause of this.According to Brent Metcalf, a certified clinical social worker in Johnson City, Tennessee, when we allow ourselves to be silent, we allow our brains to simply reset and be refreshed.This lessens the symptoms of stress and anxiety brought on by the disarray in our lives.

5. Aids in digesting information

The brain requires time to ponder, think, and rest. It needs time to organize the knowledge it already possesses and make room for the new knowledge.

You are giving your brain the time it needs to comprehend any new information by scheduling quiet time during the day.

5. Encourages creativity

In her book "Saving Our Children From Our Chaotic World: Teaching Children the Magic of Silence and Stillness," author Maggie Dent asserts that "Creativity is a huge advantage of silence and stillness." According to Dent, for the body to be in the background and the mind to be at ease, both are necessary for the zone of inspiration. Making mental space for creativity can assist.

7. Concentration aids

Dr. Elizabeth Lombardo, a psychologist in Chicago, Illinois, says that silence improves focus. "The ability to focus when the modern world and its various noises bombard your brain all at once is one of the reasons why silence has become such an important element of everyday life," states one researcher.

You might find it difficult to focus with this background noise. According to Lombardo, you might be able to concentrate better in a calm setting or one with less outside noise.

RECAP

Finding moments of stillness can have a huge positive impact on your psychological and mental health and increase your sense of tranquility.

Accepting silence can assist excite your brain and speed up information processing given all the continual noise you are exposed to daily. Additionally, it can aid in stress relief and self-awareness.

Accepting silence could also be a good way to calm your rushing thoughts and center yourself. Additionally, it can increase your creativity and help you focus better.

You can profit from stillness and enhance your mental and physical health with a little practice.

Chapter 8

How well the morning questions worked

One needs to set the aim the night before they go to bed if they want to develop or become successful with their morning routine.

The morning habits of extremely well-known and prosperous business tycoons have been the subject of numerous publications. Since July 1, 2015, I have been following the same morning routine, and it has been helpful. I accomplished all of my professional and personal goals this year as a result of this habit.

I highly suggest Hal Elrod's book The Miracle Morning. He challenges the reader to stick to a morning routine for 30 days in it. In July 2015, my book club accepted the challenge, and I have kept the tradition ever since.

I created my own set of seven nice morning questions that promote happiness that I use as an example and that I use every day.

Whatever the day's events, I always make sure to get up early enough to do my daily ritual.

Check out our extensive selection of morning texts if you're looking for a thoughtful morning message for a loved one.

To help you, here are my seven good morning questions:

1) For what do I feel grateful this morning? "Greatness begins with a grateful heart. It is an indication of modesty. It serves as a foundation for the growth of values like happiness, love, courage, satisfaction, and wellbeing. When you wake up, spend some time being thankful. When was the last time you gave all the things, people, and experiences for which you are grateful conscious consideration or verbal expression? What happens to your energy level when you start the day in this way is fantastic.

2) What positive exercise will I concentrate on this morning? Recite mantras or positive affirmations that are in line with your aspirations. By doing this, you immediately place your mind in a winning frame of mind. An incantation is defined as a written or spoken formula of words intended to have a certain outcome. An incantation is different from an affirmation in that you utilize your entire body to perform an incantation, whereas, with an affirmation, you simply say something encouraging, perhaps once or twice. On 3x5 cards, I prefer to write my incantations. I decide on one or two that work for the day.

3) How Does My Today's Schedule Look? Consider how you want your day to be. Go over your complete schedule, including how you wake up, how you get dressed, where you're going, your destination, your appointments, etc. I also prefer to concentrate on the successful outcomes of my sales appointments.

One of my favorite good morning queries is this one. Have you ever gone through a day in your head? It's fascinating and a lot of fun. I make an effort to picture every detail. I imagine myself traveling to my next location by car. What appears in the mind's eye as you go through the visualization process is extraordinary.

4) What Physical Activity Do I Want To Do This Morning?

"I exercise because it improves the quality of my life."

Spend at least 30 minutes each day working out. The workout that is most convenient for you at that moment, in my opinion, is the finest one. No specialized tools are required. Your body, mind, and spirit will all benefit immensely from a simple 30-minute walk outside in the morning.

5) What Book Am I In The Mood To Read This Morning? As exercise is to the body, reading is to the intellect. For 10 to 20 minutes, read something inspiring or motivating. While getting ready in the morning, I prefer to read a real book. Be careful not to get distracted by internet time wasters if you decide to read on portable devices.

6) What Subjects Should I Cover This Morning? Either do something worth writing about or write something worth reading. I believe that many people would benefit from journaling but lack the discipline to do so. I'm referring to writing something down with a pen or pencil. We spend so much time on technology that when we pick up a real pen and paper, I believe our brains are genuinely refreshed. I occasionally send a friend a card or letter. People appreciate receiving handwritten notes in the mail. I used the opportunity to work on writing a blog article when I first started practicing the seven good morning inquiries that lead to happiness. I discussed themes relating to business networking. Spending time on this kind of creative outlet has been gratifying for me because I adore blogging. Writing gives me a mental workout and gives me a ton of energy.

You can read my blog at Espressobrain.com if you're interested.

7) What Steps Can I Take This Morning To Learn Something New? "Find your love of learning. If you do, your growth will never stop.

Try out these seven happy-making good morning inquiries to see what happens.

This straightforward procedure can take anywhere from 30 minutes to an hour, depending on how much time is available each day. I discovered that I needed extra time to work on specific areas of my morning routine, so before getting out of bed, I set my alarm for an hour earlier. This will enable me to finish my good morning questions and give each one the appropriate attention.Though most days I can take things slow, there are occasions when I need to jam it all in. However, the most important thing is to set the intention the night before and accomplish it EVERY DAY. Even when I'm on the road or vacation, I keep up the routine. I don't let any justification stop me from beginning each day with this productive practice.

You can read my blog at [illegible] if you're interested.

What Steps Can [illegible] Take This Morning To Learn Something New? Find your love of learning; if you do, your growth will never stop.

Try out [illegible] in a copy-making [illegible] and meditate [illegible] to see what happens.

This [illegible] moving upward [illegible] because [illegible] anything [illegible] our lives [illegible] [illegible] worked [illegible] [illegible] [illegible] for an hour [illegible]. This will [illegible] to finish any good [illegible] something [illegible] and [illegible] appropriate [illegible] [illegible] can take things slow; there are occasions when I need to [illegible] however, the [illegible] important thing [illegible] and accomplish [illegible] DAY. [illegible] the [illegible] [illegible] [illegible] [illegible] [illegible] from beginning [illegible] with that ritual is practice.

www.ingramcontent.com/pod-product-compliance
Lightning Source LLC
LaVergne TN
LVHW052105160826
845678LV00015B/3373

* 9 7 9 8 8 4 5 8 5 4 3 9 1 *